WALES TRAVEL GUIDE 2023

The Ultimate Travel Guide to discover Wales: From Vibrant Cities to Majestic National Parks

RHYS HUGES

Copyright 2023 by RHYS HUGES - All rights reserved.

This document is geared towards providing exact and reliable information in regards to the topic and issue covered. The publication is sold with the idea that the publisher is not required to render accounting, officially permitted, or otherwise, qualified services. If advice is necessary, legal or professional, a practiced individual in the profession should be ordered.

From a Declaration of Principles which was accepted and approved equally by a Committee of the American Bar Association and a Committee of Publishers and Associations.

In no way is it legal to reproduce, duplicate, or transmit any part of this document in either electronic means or in printed format. Recording of this publication is strictly prohibited and any storage of this document is not allowed unless with written permission from the publisher. All rights reserved.

The information provided herein is stated to be truthful and consistent, in that any liability, in terms of inattention or otherwise, by any usage or abuse of any policies, processes, or directions contained within is the solitary and utter responsibility of the recipient reader. Under no circumstances will any legal responsibility or blame be held against the publisher for any reparation, damages, or monetary loss due to the information herein, either directly or indirectly.

Respective authors own all copyrights not held by the publisher.

The information herein is offered for informational purposes solely, and is universal as so. The presentation of the information is without contract or any type of guarantee assurance.

WALES TRAVEL GUIDE 2023

CONTENTS

WALES TRAVEL GUIDE 2023 I
CHAPTER 1 1
INTRODUCTION TO WALES 1
PRATICAL AND USEFUL TIPS TO TRAVEL TO WALES 10
CHAPTER 3 20
CARDIFF 20
CHAPTER 4 35
REGION OF NORTH WALES 35
CHAPTER 5 46
REGION OF SOUTH WALES 46
REGION OF MIDWEST WALES 56
CHAPTER 7 67
CULTURE AND LOCAL TRADITION 67
CHAPTER 8 75
TYPICAL FOOD AND DRINK 75
CHAPTER 9 84
OUTDOOR ACTIVIES 84
USEFUL NUMBERS AND CONTACT FOR THE TRIP 93

CHAPTER 1

INTRODUCTION TO WALES

1.1 Basic Information about Wales

Wales, located in the western part of the United Kingdom, is a beautiful and culturally rich country known for its stunning landscapes, historic castles, and vibrant traditions. It shares borders with England to the east and is surrounded by the Irish Sea to the north and west. The capital city of Wales is Cardiff, a dynamic and cosmopolitan metropolis that offers a blend of modern attractions and ancient landmarks. The Welsh language, known as Cymraeg, is spoken by a significant portion of the population alongside English. Wales is renowned for its rugged mountains, including Snowdon, the highest peak in the country, as well as its picturesque coastline, charming villages, and lush green valleys. With its rich history, distinct culture, and warm hospitality, Wales offers a unique and memorable travel experience for visitors from around the world.

1.2 Culture and Traditions

The culture and traditions of Wales are fascinating and deeply rooted in its rich history. Wales has a strong cultural identity, and its people take great pride in their heritage. The Welsh language, known as Cymraeg, plays a significant role in preserving and promoting Welsh culture. Traditional music, poetry, and storytelling are cherished art forms that have been passed down through generations. The Eisteddfod, a festival celebrating Welsh literature, music, and performance, is a highlight of the cultural calendar. Wales is also renowned for its passionate love of rugby, with international matches evoking a sense of national pride and unity. The country's folklore is filled with mythical tales of dragons and legendary figures like King Arthur. Traditional costumes, such as the iconic Welsh national costume, showcase the vibrant and distinctive Welsh aesthetic. Furthermore, the annual celebration of St. David's Day on March 1st, honoring the patron saint of Wales, is a significant cultural event where people proudly display daffodils and leeks, national emblems of Wales. These cultural elements combine to create a unique and enchanting experience for both locals and visitors alike.

In addition to its language and folklore, Wales also boasts a rich tradition of arts and crafts. Skilled artisans create intricate tapestries, pottery, and wooden carvings, showcasing the country's craftsmanship and creativity. Traditional festivals like Calan Mai (May Day) and Noson Gyflaith (Toffee Evening) bring communities together to celebrate with music, dancing, and delicious traditional foods. The close connection to nature is another important aspect of Welsh culture, with the Welsh landscape serving as inspiration for many artists and writers. The country's stunning national parks, such as Snowdonia and Brecon Beacons, offer opportunities for outdoor activities like hiking, mountain biking, and exploring ancient ruins. The concept of "hiraeth" holds a special place in Welsh culture, reflecting a deep longing for one's homeland and a sense of nostalgia for the Welsh way of life. Overall, the culture and traditions of Wales are woven into the fabric of everyday life, preserving a rich heritage while embracing contemporary influences and ensuring a vibrant and evolving cultural scene.

Here are some historical figures from Wales who have made a significant impact:

1. Owain Glyndŵr (1359-1415): Owain Glyndŵr was a Welsh prince who led a rebellion against English rule in the early 15th century. He is considered a national hero in Wales and is remembered for his efforts to restore Welsh independence.
2. Llywelyn the Great (1173-1240): Llywelyn ap Iorwerth, commonly known as Llywelyn the Great, was a powerful medieval prince who ruled over much of Wales during the 13th century. He successfully expanded and consolidated Welsh territories and is regarded as one of the greatest Welsh rulers.
3. Saint David (c. 500-589): Saint David, or Dewi Sant in Welsh, is the patron saint of Wales. He was a 6th-century bishop who founded several monastic settlements and played a crucial role in spreading Christianity in Wales.
4. Henry Tudor (1457-1509): Henry Tudor, born in Wales, became King Henry VII of England after his victory at the Battle of Bosworth in 1485. He established the Tudor dynasty and brought about political stability, laying the foundation for the English Renaissance.

5. Aneurin Bevan (1897-1960): Aneurin Bevan was a Welsh politician and a key figure in the establishment of the National Health Service (NHS) in the United Kingdom. He served as the Minister of Health in the post-World War II Labour government and is revered for his contribution to healthcare accessibility.
6. Roald Dahl (1916-1990): Although born in Wales, Roald Dahl achieved worldwide fame as a celebrated children's author. His imaginative and whimsical stories, including "Charlie and the Chocolate Factory" and "Matilda," have captivated generations of readers.

These historical figures have left a lasting legacy, shaping Welsh history, culture, and identity.

1.3 What to Expect During Your Trip

When traveling to Wales, you can expect a unique and captivating experience. Here are some things to anticipate during your trip:
1. Breathtaking Landscapes: Wales is known for its stunning natural beauty. From majestic mountains and rolling hills to dramatic coastlines and serene lakes, the Welsh landscape offers a diverse range of breathtaking scenery. Be prepared to encounter picturesque countryside, charming villages, and opportunities for outdoor adventures.

2. Rich History and Castles: Wales boasts a wealth of historical sites and medieval castles. You can explore ancient fortresses like Caernarfon Castle, Conwy Castle, and Cardiff Castle, which provide a glimpse into the country's fascinating past. The ruins of ancient abbeys and monastic sites also dot the landscape, offering insights into Wales' religious heritage.

3. Vibrant Cultural Heritage: Welsh culture is vibrant and distinctive. You can immerse yourself in the Welsh language, traditional music, and folklore. Look forward to attending lively festivals, such as the Eisteddfod, where you can witness poetry recitals, music performances, and traditional Welsh competitions. Try experiencing a traditional Welsh choir or listening to a talented harpist.

4. Outdoor Adventures: With its vast national parks and extensive coastline, Wales is an ideal destination for outdoor enthusiasts. Prepare for thrilling activities like hiking, cycling, mountain biking, and water sports. Whether you choose to conquer the peaks of Snowdonia National Park or explore the coastal paths of Pembrokeshire, there are countless opportunities to enjoy nature and adventure.

5. Warm Welsh Hospitality: The Welsh are known for their friendliness and warm hospitality. You can expect a warm welcome and genuine interactions with locals. Don't hesitate to strike up conversations and learn more about

the local culture and traditions.

6. Delicious Culinary Delights: Welsh cuisine offers a delightful fusion of traditional and modern flavors. Look forward to trying traditional dishes such as Welsh rarebit (a savory cheese toast), cawl (a hearty soup), and bara brith (a fruit loaf). You can also sample local cheeses, seafood, and artisanal products. Don't forget to indulge in a traditional Welsh afternoon tea or enjoy a pint of locally brewed beer.

Overall, traveling to Wales promises a blend of natural beauty, rich history, cultural immersion, and warm hospitality, ensuring a memorable and rewarding experience for visitors.

WALES TRAVEL GUIDE 2023

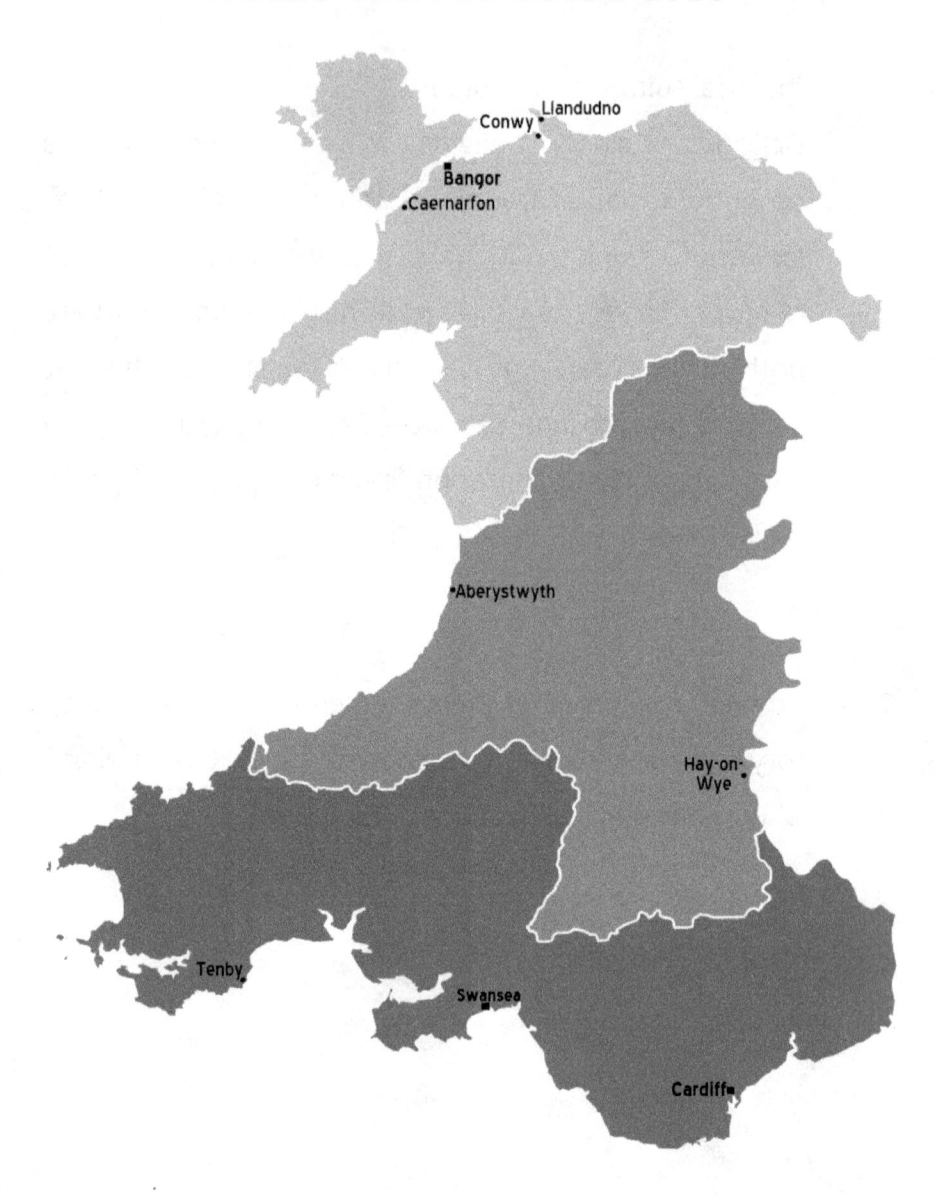

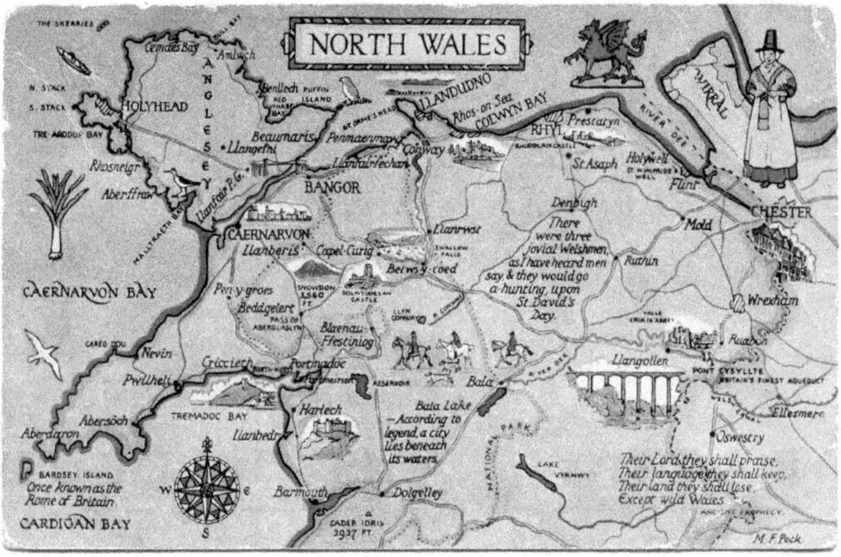
NORTH WALES
THE SKERRIES
Cemaes Bay
Amlwch
ANGLESEY
N. STACK
S. STACK
HOLYHEAD
Benllech
PUFFIN ISLAND
RED WHARF BAY
Beaumaris
Llangefni
Rhosneigr
Aberffraw
Llanfair P.G.
MALLTRAETH BAY
Penmaenmawr
Llanfairfechan
BANGOR
CAERNARVON
Llanberis
Capel Curig
CAERNARVON BAY
Pen-y-groes
Beddgelert
SNOWDON 3,560 FT.
PASS OF ABERGLASLYN
Blaenau Ffestiniog
Nevin
Criccieth
Portmadoc
Pwllheli
RESERVOIR
TREMADOC BAY
Harlech
Abersoch
Aberdaron
Llanbedr
BARDSEY ISLAND
Once known as the Rome of Britain
W
E
S
CARDIGAN BAY
Barmouth
Dolgelley
CADER IDRIS 2927 FT.
LLANDUDNO
Rhos-on-Sea
COLWYN BAY
Conway
RHYL
Prestatyn
St Asaph
Holywell
ST WINEFRIDE'S WELL
Flint
RIVER DEE
WIRRAL
CHESTER
Denbigh
Llanrwst
SWALLOW FALLS
Betws-y-coed
There were three jovial Welshmen, as I have heard men say, & they would go a-hunting, upon St David's Day.
Mold
Ruthin
Wrexham
Ruabon
Llangollen
PONT CYSYLLTE
BRITAIN'S FINEST AQUEDUCT
Ellesmere
Oswestry
Bala
RIVER DEE
Bala Lake
—According to legend, a city lies beneath its waters.
NATIONAL PARK
LAKE VYRNWY
Their Lord they shall praise,
Their language they shall keep,
Their land they shall lose,
Except wild Wales.
M. F. Peck

CHAPTER 2

PRATICAL AND USEFUL TIPS TO TRAVEL TO WALES

If you are traveling from Europe or America to Wales, there are certain travel documents and requirements to keep in mind:

1. Passport: Ensure that your passport is valid for the duration of your stay in Wales. Check the expiration date and make sure you have at least six months' validity remaining on your passport.
2. Visa: If you are a citizen of the European Union (EU) or European Economic Area (EEA), you generally do not need a visa to enter Wales. The same applies to citizens of the United States, Canada, Australia, and many other countries who can visit Wales for tourism purposes for up to 90 days without a visa. However, it is always advisable

to check the visa requirements based on your nationality before traveling.

3. COVID-19 Requirements: Due to the ongoing COVID-19 pandemic, there may be additional travel requirements and restrictions in place. Check the latest travel advisories and guidelines from the Welsh government and the country you are traveling from. This may include providing proof of vaccination, negative COVID-19 tests, or completing health declaration forms. Stay updated on any quarantine or self-isolation requirements as well.

4. Travel Insurance: It is recommended to have travel insurance that covers medical expenses and trip cancellation or interruption. Check your insurance policy to ensure it provides adequate coverage for your trip to Wales.

5. Driving License: If you plan to rent a car and drive in Wales, check if your driving license is valid and accepted. In general, driving licenses from EU and EEA countries are valid in Wales. Non-EU and non-EEA citizens may need an International Driving Permit (IDP) along with their valid driving license.

It is crucial to research and verify the specific requirements based on your country of origin and current travel regulations. Contact the nearest embassy or consulate of the United Kingdom for the most up-to-date information and guidance regarding travel documents and requirements

The best time to visit Wales depends on your preferences and the activities you plan to engage in. Here are some considerations for different seasons in Wales:

1. Spring (March to May): Spring in Wales brings milder temperatures, blooming flowers, and lush green landscapes. It's a great time for outdoor activities like hiking and exploring gardens. However, be prepared for occasional rain showers.
2. Summer (June to August): Summer is the peak tourist season in Wales. The weather is generally pleasant, with longer daylight hours and average temperatures ranging from 15 to 25 degrees Celsius (59 to 77 degrees Fahrenheit). It's an ideal time for exploring coastal areas, visiting castles, and enjoying outdoor festivals and events.
3. Autumn (September to November): Autumn in Wales offers beautiful foliage colors and quieter tourist crowds. The temperatures start to cool down, ranging from 10 to 20 degrees Celsius (50 to 68 degrees Fahrenheit). It's a great time for scenic drives, walking trails, and exploring historical sites.

4. Winter (December to February): Winter in Wales is characterized by cooler temperatures, with averages ranging from 2 to 8 degrees Celsius (36 to 46 degrees Fahrenheit). It's a quieter season, and you can enjoy festive markets, cozy countryside retreats, and winter sports in places like Snowdonia National Park.

It's worth noting that Wales has a maritime climate, which means the weather can be changeable and rain showers can occur throughout the year. It's advisable to pack layers and waterproof clothing regardless of the season.

Ultimately, the best time to visit Wales depends on your interests and the type of experience you seek. Consider the weather, activities, and the level of tourist crowds to choose the most suitable time for your visit.

2.3 Transportation in Wales

When traveling in Wales, you have several transportation options to explore the country:

1. Trains: Wales has an extensive rail network that connects major cities and towns, making it a convenient mode of transportation. The main train operator in Wales is Transport for Wales, offering services to destinations within Wales and connecting with other parts of the United

Kingdom.

2. Buses: Buses are a popular and economical way to travel within Wales. Local bus services operate in cities and towns, providing easy access to various attractions. National Express and Megabus also offer long-distance coach services to and from Wales.

3. Cars: Renting a car gives you the flexibility to explore Wales at your own pace, especially if you plan to venture into rural areas or remote regions. The road network in Wales is well-maintained, and there are scenic driving routes that allow you to experience the country's natural beauty. Just keep in mind that driving in cities may involve traffic and parking challenges.

4. Ferries: If you plan to travel to Wales from Ireland, there are ferry services available from ports such as Dublin and Rosslare to Holyhead and Fishguard in Wales. Ferries provide a scenic and enjoyable way to reach Wales, with the option to bring your vehicle or travel as a foot passenger.

5. Airports: Wales has several airports that connect to domestic and international destinations. Cardiff Airport is the largest airport in Wales, offering flights to various European destinations. Other regional airports include Anglesey, Swansea, and Aberporth, serving domestic flights and occasional charter services.

6. Walking and Cycling: Wales is a great destination for

walkers and cyclists, with an extensive network of trails and paths. You can explore the countryside, national parks, and coastal routes on foot or by bike, immersing yourself in the natural beauty of Wales.

Public transportation in Wales is generally reliable, but it's advisable to check schedules and plan your journeys in advance, especially if you have specific time constraints. Remember to consider any COVID-19-related restrictions or guidelines that may affect public transportation services during your visit.

2.4 Practical Tips for Traveling:

When traveling to Wales, consider the following practical tips to enhance your trip:

1. Weather and Clothing: Wales has a maritime climate, so be prepared for changing weather conditions. Pack clothing layers to accommodate varying temperatures and consider waterproof outerwear. It's a good idea to carry an umbrella or raincoat as well.
2. Currency: The currency used in Wales is the British Pound (GBP). It's advisable to have some cash on hand for small expenses, as not all places may accept cards. ATMs are widely available in cities and towns for withdrawing cash.
3. Electrical Outlets: Wales uses the standard UK three-pin

electrical outlets. If your electronic devices use a different plug type, bring an adapter to ensure you can charge your devices.

4. Safety: Wales is generally a safe destination for travelers, but it's always wise to take precautions. Keep your valuables secure, be aware of your surroundings, and follow any local safety guidelines. If hiking or engaging in outdoor activities, inform someone about your plans and take necessary precautions.

5. Wi-Fi and Communication: Most hotels, restaurants, and public places in Wales offer Wi-Fi access. If you need constant internet connectivity, consider purchasing a local SIM card or using portable Wi-Fi devices. Check with your service provider for international roaming options and charges.

6. Travel Insurance: It is strongly recommended to have travel insurance that covers medical emergencies, trip cancellation or interruption, and personal belongings. Review your insurance policy to ensure it provides adequate coverage for your needs.

7. Local Customs and Etiquette: Familiarize yourself with basic local customs and etiquette. Politeness and respect are valued in Welsh culture. When visiting religious sites or private properties, adhere to any guidelines or dress codes.

8. Plan and Book in Advance: To ensure availability and the

best prices, consider booking accommodations, attractions, and transportation in advance, especially during peak travel seasons.
9. Tipping: Tipping in Wales is not mandatory, but it is customary to leave a gratuity for good service. In restaurants, a 10% to 15% tip is appreciated if service charge is not included.
10. COVID-19 Considerations: Stay updated on the latest travel advisories, health guidelines, and COVID-19-related requirements for Wales. Check entry requirements, quarantine regulations, and any restrictions that may affect your travel plans.

By keeping these practical tips in mind, you can have a smoother and more enjoyable travel experience in Wales.

When traveling to Wales, there are several airports and airlines that you can consider for your journey. Here are some recommended airports and airlines for your convenience:

1. Cardiff Airport (CWL): Located in the capital city of Wales, Cardiff Airport is the largest airport in the country. It offers domestic and international flights, connecting Wales to

various destinations in Europe and beyond. Airlines operating at Cardiff Airport include Flybe, KLM, Ryanair, and TUI Airways.

2. Bristol Airport (BRS): While not in Wales, Bristol Airport is located just across the border in England and is a convenient option for accessing South Wales. It offers a wide range of domestic and international flights, including connections to major European cities. Airlines operating at Bristol Airport include easyJet, Ryanair, and TUI Airways.

3. Manchester Airport (MAN): Situated in England, Manchester Airport is another viable option for accessing Wales, especially for those visiting the northern parts of the country. It is a major international airport with a wide range of airlines and flight connections. Airlines operating at Manchester Airport include British Airways, easyJet, Ryanair, and Flybe.

4. Liverpool John Lennon Airport (LPL): Although located in England, Liverpool John Lennon Airport is within reasonable distance to parts of North Wales. It offers domestic and international flights, with airlines such as easyJet, Ryanair, and Wizz Air serving various destinations.

When choosing an airline, consider factors such as flight availability, pricing, baggage allowances, and overall customer service. It's advisable to compare different airlines, check their reviews, and book your tickets in advance to secure the best deals.

Additionally, remember to check the specific airports' websites for up-to-date information on flight schedules, services, and any COVID-19-related guidelines or requirements that may be in place during your travel period.

CHAPTER 3

CARDIFF

3.1 Overview of Cardiff:

Cardiff, the capital city of Wales, offers a vibrant blend of history, culture, and modern amenities. Here's an overview of what you can expect when visiting Cardiff:

1. Cardiff Castle: A must-visit attraction, Cardiff Castle showcases a mix of architectural styles from Roman to Gothic Revival. Explore the medieval keep, extravagant

interiors, and wander through the beautiful parkland surrounding the castle.

2. Cardiff Bay: This waterfront area has undergone significant redevelopment and is now a bustling hub of entertainment, dining, and cultural attractions. Visit the Wales Millennium Centre, home to performing arts, or take a boat tour around the bay to enjoy stunning views and learn about its maritime history.

3. Principality Stadium: Known for hosting major sporting events, including rugby matches and concerts, the Principality Stadium is an iconic landmark in Cardiff. Even if you can't catch a live event, you can take a guided tour to explore the impressive stadium and learn about its history.

4. National Museum Cardiff: Immerse yourself in art, natural history, and archaeology at the National Museum Cardiff. The museum houses a diverse collection of exhibits, including works by Welsh and international artists, fossils, and ancient artifacts.

5. Shopping and Dining: Cardiff offers excellent shopping opportunities, with a mix of high-street stores, independent boutiques, and bustling markets. Head to St. David's Cardiff, one of the largest shopping centers in the UK, or explore the vibrant arcades for unique finds. When it comes to dining, you'll find a wide range of cuisine

options, from traditional Welsh dishes to international flavors.

6. Parks and Gardens: Cardiff boasts several green spaces where you can relax and enjoy nature. Bute Park, located near Cardiff Castle, offers tranquil gardens, meandering paths, and beautiful views of the castle and river. Roath Park, with its expansive lake and Victorian conservatory, is another popular spot for leisurely strolls.

7. Cultural Events: Cardiff hosts numerous cultural events throughout the year. Keep an eye out for festivals, concerts, and theatrical performances, especially at the Wales Millennium Centre and various venues across the city.

8. Sports and Recreation: As the capital of Welsh rugby, Cardiff has a strong sports culture. Catch a rugby match at the Principality Stadium or visit Cardiff International White Water for thrilling water sports activities. The city also offers plenty of opportunities for cycling, walking, and exploring the Taff Trail.

With its rich history, cultural attractions, vibrant city life, and warm Welsh hospitality, Cardiff offers a captivating experience for visitors.

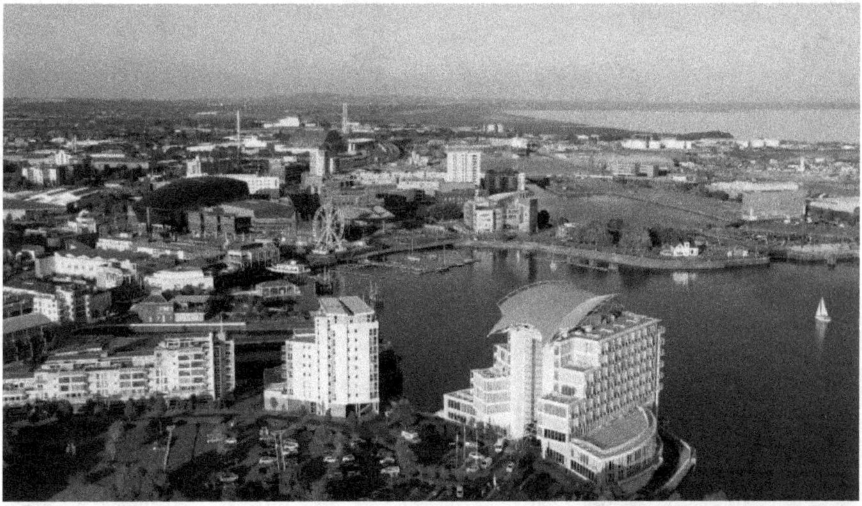

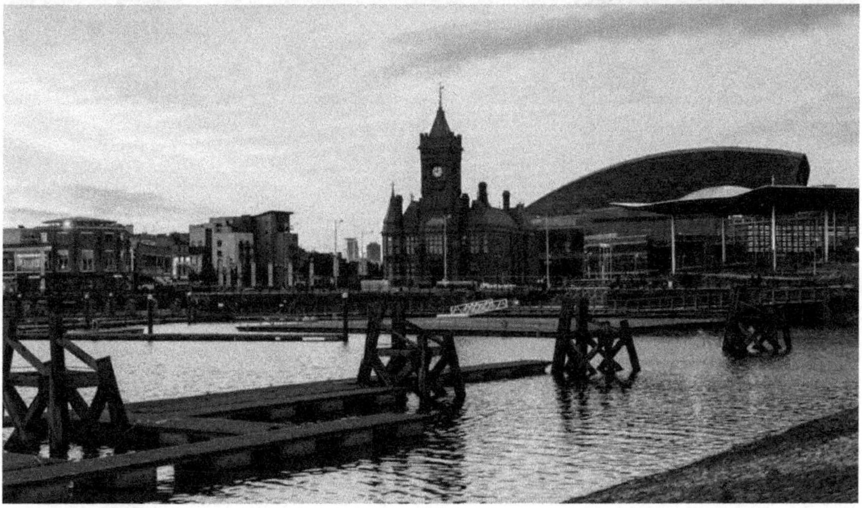

WALES TRAVEL GUIDE 2023

RHYS HUGES

WALES TRAVEL GUIDE 2023

Here are some of the top tourist attractions in Cardiff:
1. Cardiff Castle: This magnificent castle, located in the heart of the city, is a blend of Roman, Norman, and Gothic architecture. Explore the lavish interiors, climb the keep for panoramic views, and wander through the enchanting castle grounds.
2. Cardiff Bay: A vibrant waterfront area, Cardiff Bay offers a mix of entertainment, dining, and cultural attractions. Visit the Wales Millennium Centre, an iconic arts venue, or take a boat tour to discover the bay's maritime history. Don't miss the stunning Norwegian Church and the Doctor Who Experience.
3. National Museum Cardiff: Immerse yourself in art, history, and natural sciences at this impressive museum. Marvel at the diverse collection of art, including works by Welsh and international artists, and explore the archaeological and natural history exhibits.
4. St. Fagans National Museum of History: Located just outside Cardiff, this open-air museum offers a fascinating glimpse into Welsh history and culture. Explore over 40

historic buildings, including traditional houses, a working farm, and a medieval church, all set in beautiful parkland.

5. Cardiff Bay Barrage: Take a leisurely stroll along the Cardiff Bay Barrage, a promenade that connects Cardiff Bay to Penarth. Enjoy panoramic views of the bay, the Bristol Channel, and the city skyline. The barrage also provides a great spot for picnics and outdoor activities.

6. Principality Stadium: Known for its impressive architecture and as the home of Welsh rugby, the Principality Stadium is a must-visit for sports enthusiasts. Take a guided tour to explore the stadium, walk through the players' tunnel, and learn about its history.

7. Llandaff Cathedral: Visit this stunning cathedral, dedicated to St. Peter and St. Paul, located in the Llandaff district of Cardiff. Admire the beautiful Gothic architecture, intricate stained glass windows, and peaceful surroundings.

8. Cardiff Market: Step into the bustling Cardiff Market, where you'll find a variety of stalls offering fresh produce, local delicacies, artisan crafts, and more. It's a great place to shop for souvenirs and experience the lively atmosphere of a traditional market.

These are just a few of the many attractions Cardiff has to offer. Whether you're interested in history, culture, sports, or simply enjoying the vibrant city life, Cardiff has something for everyone.

3.3 Traditional Food and Restaurants in Cardiff:

When it comes to food, Cardiff offers a diverse culinary scene with a mix of traditional Welsh dishes and international flavors. Here are some typical Welsh foods to try and recommended restaurants in Cardiff:

1. Welsh Cawl: A hearty traditional Welsh soup made with lamb or beef, root vegetables, and leeks. It's a warming and flavorful dish often enjoyed during colder months. Try it at The Potted Pig, a restaurant known for its modern Welsh cuisine.
2. Welsh Rarebit: A classic Welsh dish consisting of a savory cheese sauce served over toasted bread. It's a delicious and satisfying snack or light meal. Sample it at The Clink Restaurant, located within Cardiff Prison and offering a unique dining experience while supporting prisoner rehabilitation.
3. Glamorgan Sausages: These vegetarian sausages are made with a mixture of cheese, breadcrumbs, leeks, and herbs, coated in breadcrumbs and fried until golden. You can find them at various traditional pubs and restaurants like The Lansdowne Pub.
4. Laverbread: A traditional Welsh delicacy made from

seaweed that is harvested along the coast. It is often served as part of a traditional Welsh breakfast or as a topping for dishes like Welsh rarebit. Look for it at The Classroom, a restaurant that celebrates local ingredients and Welsh culinary traditions.

5. Bara Brith: A delicious fruit loaf made with tea-soaked dried fruits, spices, and sometimes a touch of honey or marmalade. It's a popular treat served with butter or enjoyed as part of afternoon tea. Find it at Pettigrew Tea Rooms, a charming tearoom located in the heart of Bute Park.

6. International Cuisine: Cardiff also boasts a wide range of international restaurants, reflecting its multicultural atmosphere. From Indian and Italian to Chinese and Mexican, you'll find a diverse selection of flavors to suit every palate. Explore City Road, known for its variety of international restaurants.

7. Cardiff Central Market: For a taste of local produce and traditional Welsh treats, visit Cardiff Central Market. You'll find stalls offering Welsh cheeses, meats, pastries, and more. Don't miss the famous local bakery, Clark's Pies, known for their savory meat-filled pastries.

These are just a few examples of the traditional Welsh foods and recommended restaurants in Cardiff. The city's culinary scene is constantly evolving, so be sure to explore and try different establishments to discover your own favorite flavors and dining experiences.

3.4 Nightlife and Entertainment in Cardiff:

Cardiff offers a vibrant and diverse nightlife scene, with a range of options for entertainment, dining, and socializing. Here are some highlights of the nightlife and entertainment in Cardiff:

1. Cardiff Bay: The waterfront area of Cardiff Bay is a popular destination for nightlife. Enjoy a drink at one of the stylish bars or waterfront pubs while taking in the scenic views. The area also offers live music venues and clubs for those looking to dance the night away.
2. St. Mary Street and Mill Lane: These bustling streets in the city center are lined with a variety of bars, clubs, and pubs. You'll find everything from traditional pubs serving local ales to trendy cocktail bars and lively nightclubs. It's a hub for nightlife and a great place to experience Cardiff's buzzing atmosphere.

3. Live Music: Cardiff has a thriving live music scene, with numerous venues hosting both local and international artists. The Motorpoint Arena Cardiff and Tramshed are popular concert venues that attract big-name acts, while smaller venues like Clwb Ifor Bach and The Globe showcase local talent and up-and-coming bands.

4. Theatres and Performing Arts: Cardiff is home to several theatres and performing arts venues, offering a wide range of shows and performances. The Wales Millennium Centre is a prominent venue for theatre, opera, and ballet productions. Other notable venues include the New Theatre and Chapter Arts Centre, which showcase a variety of performances, including drama, comedy, and dance.

5. Comedy Clubs: If you're in the mood for laughter, Cardiff has several comedy clubs where you can enjoy stand-up comedy acts. The Glee Club Cardiff and The Comedy Store at The Cornerhouse are popular venues that regularly host comedy nights featuring both established and emerging comedians.

6. Cinemas: Cardiff has several cinemas where you can catch the latest films. Cineworld Cardiff and Vue Cardiff are two major multiplex cinemas offering a wide selection of movies, while Chapter Arts Centre often screens independent and art-house films.

7. Casinos: For those looking for a bit of excitement, Cardiff

has a few casinos where you can try your luck at card games, roulette, or slot machines. Rainbow Casino and Grosvenor Casino Cardiff are two popular options for a night of entertainment and gaming.

8. Festivals and Events: Cardiff hosts various festivals and events throughout the year, ranging from cultural celebrations to food and drink festivals. Keep an eye out for events like Cardiff Festival, Cardiff Food and Drink Festival, and the Welsh Proms, which showcase the city's vibrant cultural scene.

Whether you're into live music, comedy, theatre, or simply enjoying a night out, Cardiff offers a lively and diverse nightlife that caters to different tastes and interests.

WALES TRAVEL GUIDE 2023

CHAPTER 4

REGION OF NORTH WALES

4.1 Snowdonia National Park:

Snowdonia National Park, located in the northwest of Wales, is a breathtakingly beautiful and diverse natural paradise. Here's a detailed paragraph about Snowdonia National Park:

Snowdonia National Park is a haven for nature lovers and outdoor enthusiasts. Spanning over 823 square miles (2,130 square kilometers), it is home to stunning landscapes, rugged mountains, picturesque lakes, and ancient woodlands. The park's centerpiece is Mount Snowdon, the highest peak in Wales and England, offering panoramic views from its summit.

Hiking and climbing opportunities abound in Snowdonia, with numerous trails catering to all levels of experience. The popular Llanberis Path provides a gradual ascent to the summit of Snowdon, while more challenging routes like the Pyg Track and the Watkin Path offer thrilling adventures for experienced hikers. The park also boasts a network of mountain biking trails, providing thrilling rides through the stunning countryside.

Snowdonia is dotted with sparkling lakes and tranquil reservoirs, such as Llyn Tegid (Bala Lake) and Llyn Padarn, offering opportunities for boating, fishing, and leisurely walks along the shorelines. The cascading waterfalls of Swallow Falls and Aber Falls add to the park's natural splendor.

Wildlife enthusiasts will appreciate the diverse flora and fauna of Snowdonia. The park is home to rare and protected species, including the majestic red kite and the elusive otter. Keep an eye out for birds of prey, such as peregrine falcons and buzzards, soaring above the rugged terrain. The ancient oak woodlands provide habitats for various woodland birds and a rich display of wildflowers in the spring and summer months.

In addition to its natural wonders, Snowdonia is steeped in history and culture. The charming village of Betws-y-Coed serves as a gateway to the park and offers quaint shops, tea rooms, and traditional pubs. The narrow-gauge Welsh Highland Railway takes visitors on a scenic journey through the park, offering breathtaking views along the way. The heritage sites of Harlech Castle and Caernarfon Castle, both UNESCO World Heritage Sites, provide a glimpse into Wales' medieval past.

Accommodation options in Snowdonia range from cozy bed and breakfasts to luxury hotels and self-catering cottages, catering to different budgets and preferences. Campsites and caravan parks are also available for those who prefer a closer connection to nature.

Whether you're seeking thrilling outdoor adventures, peaceful walks in nature, or a glimpse into Wales' rich history and culture, Snowdonia National Park offers a truly unforgettable experience.

4.2 Conwy and its Castle:

Conwy, a historic town located on the North Wales coast, is renowned for its well-preserved medieval walls and impressive

Conwy Castle. Here's a detailed paragraph about Conwy and its castle:

Nestled on the banks of the River Conwy, the town of Conwy is a treasure trove of history and charm. Its most iconic landmark is Conwy Castle, a majestic fortress that dominates the skyline. Built by Edward I in the 13th century as part of his ring of castles to subdue the Welsh, Conwy Castle is a UNESCO World Heritage Site and one of the finest examples of medieval military architecture in Europe.

The castle's imposing walls and towers still stand tall, providing breathtaking views of the surrounding countryside and the town itself. Exploring the castle's interiors, you'll find an array of well-preserved features, including the Great Hall, the King's Apartments, and the Queen's Chamber. The castle's strategic position on a rocky outcrop overlooking the river and the town showcases its military significance in medieval times.

Beyond the castle, Conwy offers a delightful mix of narrow cobbled streets, historic buildings, and quaint shops. Stroll along the town walls, which encircle the entire town and offer scenic views of the surrounding area. The 14th-century Aberconwy House, now a National Trust property, provides a glimpse into Conwy's past with its period rooms and exhibits.

Conwy's medieval streets are lined with charming shops, tea rooms, and traditional pubs. Explore the bustling quayside and sample fresh seafood or enjoy a traditional Welsh afternoon tea. The town's vibrant atmosphere and friendly locals make it a welcoming place to spend some time.

For history enthusiasts, Plas Mawr, a beautifully restored Elizabethan townhouse, is a must-visit. Step back in time as you wander through its intricately decorated rooms, discovering the opulent lifestyle of the Elizabethan era.

Conwy's location also makes it an excellent base for exploring the surrounding area. The Great Orme, a striking limestone headland, offers stunning views of Conwy Bay and is home to a nature reserve and a tramway that takes you to the summit. The nearby Bodnant Garden is a paradise for nature lovers, with its manicured gardens, vibrant flowers, and peaceful walks.

With its rich history, well-preserved architecture, and stunning castle, Conwy offers a captivating glimpse into medieval Wales. Whether you're interested in history, scenic beauty, or simply soaking up the charming atmosphere, a visit to Conwy and its castle is sure to leave a lasting impression.

4.3 Anglesey and its Coastline:

Anglesey, located off the northwest coast of Wales, is an enchanting island known for its stunning coastline, picturesque landscapes, and rich history. Here's a detailed paragraph about Anglesey and its coastline:

Anglesey is a captivating island that boasts a diverse and scenic coastline, making it a paradise for nature enthusiasts and beach lovers. The island is surrounded by the Irish Sea, offering a plethora of beautiful sandy beaches, rocky coves, and dramatic cliffs. From the expansive sands of Newborough Beach to the hidden gems of Porth Dafarch and Llanddwyn Bay, there's a beach to suit every preference.

One of Anglesey's most iconic features is its rugged coastal path, which stretches for approximately 125 miles (201 kilometers) and provides breathtaking views at every turn. The path takes you along towering cliffs, secluded bays, and charming fishing villages. It's an ideal route for walkers and hikers who want to explore the island's stunning coastal scenery.

The coastline of Anglesey is also rich in wildlife and offers opportunities for birdwatching and seal spotting. The island is a haven for seabirds, and during the breeding season, you can witness colonies of puffins, guillemots, and razorbills nesting on the cliffs. Keep an eye out for dolphins and seals, which can often be spotted swimming in the surrounding waters.

Anglesey's coastal areas are dotted with historic landmarks and attractions. Beaumaris, a picturesque town on the eastern coast, is home to Beaumaris Castle, a UNESCO World Heritage Site. This magnificent medieval fortress is renowned for its concentric design and is one of the finest examples of Edwardian architecture in Britain. The town itself offers charming streets lined with independent shops, cafes, and restaurants.

Further along the coast, you'll find the South Stack Lighthouse, perched on a dramatic cliff edge. Take a walk down the 400 steps to the lighthouse and marvel at the breathtaking views across the sea. Nearby, the RSPB South Stack Cliffs Nature Reserve is a paradise for birdwatchers, with a variety of seabirds nesting on the cliffs.

Anglesey's coastline also offers opportunities for water-based activities, such as kayaking, sailing, and windsurfing. The sheltered waters of the Menai Strait provide ideal conditions for these activities, while the strong currents around the island's northern coast attract surfers looking for an adrenaline rush.

With its stunning beaches, dramatic cliffs, rich wildlife, and historic landmarks, Anglesey's coastline is a true gem. Whether you're seeking relaxation on pristine sands, exhilarating coastal walks, or encounters with nature, Anglesey's coastal beauty will leave you captivated and longing to return.

4.4 Bangor and its Surroundings:

Bangor, a vibrant city located in North Wales, offers a mix of historical charm, natural beauty, and cultural attractions. Here's a detailed paragraph about Bangor and its surroundings:

Bangor is a bustling city with a rich history and a picturesque setting on the Menai Strait. The city is known for its historic

Bangor Cathedral, which dates back to the 6th century and boasts stunning architecture and beautiful grounds. Take a stroll through the cathedral's tranquil gardens and admire its intricate stained glass windows.

Surrounded by stunning natural landscapes, Bangor serves as an excellent base for exploring the nearby attractions. Just a short distance away, you'll find the breathtaking Snowdonia National Park, with its majestic mountains, tranquil lakes, and scenic hiking trails. Outdoor enthusiasts can enjoy activities like mountain biking, rock climbing, and kayaking amidst the park's stunning beauty.

Another notable attraction near Bangor is the UNESCO World Heritage site of Pontcysyllte Aqueduct. This impressive feat of engineering, located in the nearby town of Wrexham, carries the Llangollen Canal over the River Dee and offers stunning views from its towering structure.

If you're interested in Welsh history, a visit to the nearby Penrhyn Castle is a must. This magnificent neo-Norman castle is set amidst beautiful gardens and offers a glimpse into the opulent lifestyle of the Victorian era. Explore its grand rooms, stroll through the expansive grounds, and learn about the castle's fascinating history.

For those seeking coastal beauty, Anglesey, just a short drive from Bangor, offers stunning beaches, charming seaside villages, and historic landmarks. Visit the picturesque town of Beaumaris and explore its medieval castle, or relax on the sandy shores of Red

Wharf Bay. The island is also home to the iconic South Stack Lighthouse, which offers breathtaking views and opportunities for birdwatching.

Back in Bangor, the city itself offers a vibrant arts and culture scene. The Pontio Arts and Innovation Centre showcases a diverse range of performances, exhibitions, and events throughout the year. The city's high street is lined with a mix of independent boutiques, cafes, and traditional pubs, where you can soak up the local atmosphere and sample delicious Welsh cuisine.

With its combination of historical landmarks, proximity to stunning natural landscapes, and a thriving cultural scene, Bangor and its surroundings offer a wealth of experiences for visitors. Whether you're interested in history, outdoor adventures, or simply immersing yourself in the beauty of North Wales, Bangor is a destination that has something for everyone.

WALES TRAVEL GUIDE 2023

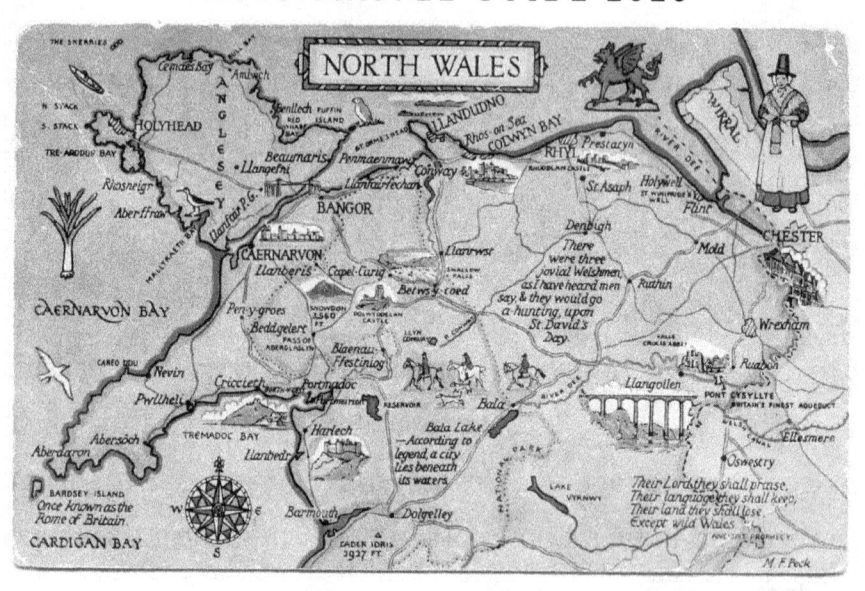

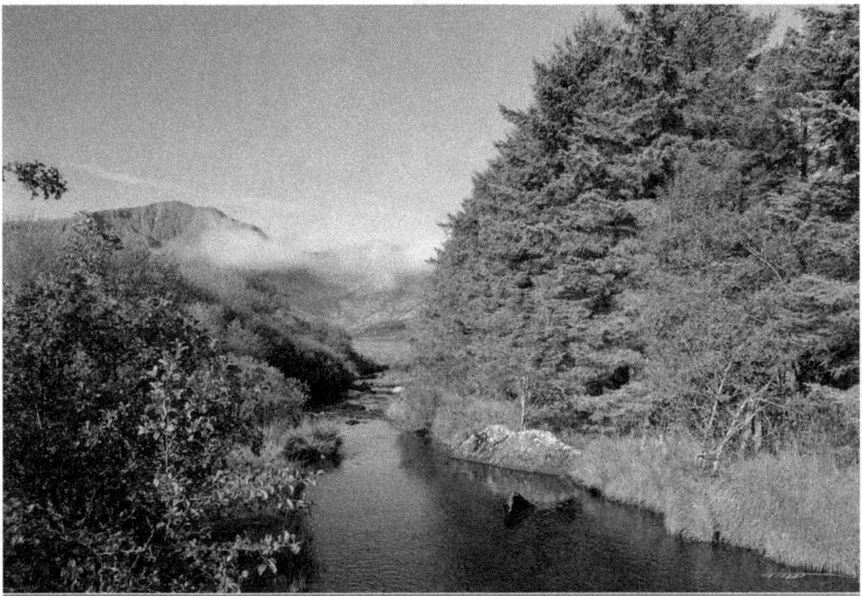

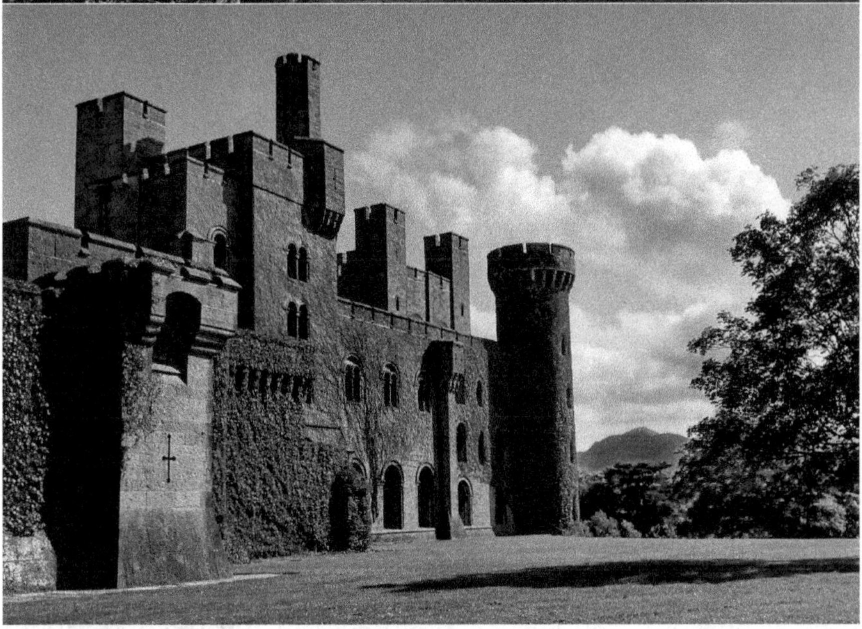

CHAPTER 5

REGION OF SOUTH WALES

5.1 Brecon Beacons National Park:

Brecon Beacons National Park, situated in the heart of South Wales, is a captivating and diverse landscape renowned for its rolling hills, dramatic mountains, and picturesque valleys. Here's a detailed paragraph about Brecon Beacons National Park:

Brecon Beacons National Park covers an expansive area of approximately 520 square miles (1,347 square kilometers), offering a haven for outdoor enthusiasts and nature lovers. The park is characterized by its distinct natural features, including the iconic Brecon Beacons mountain range, which provides a stunning backdrop to the surrounding countryside.

The park's peaks, such as Pen y Fan and Corn Du, attract hikers and climbers from near and far. These mountains offer breathtaking views from their summits, rewarding those who conquer their heights with sweeping panoramas of the rolling landscapes below. There are various trails and routes catering to different levels of experience, from gentle walks to challenging ascents.

The valleys within the national park are equally enchanting, with their picturesque villages, meandering rivers, and lush green pastures. The Usk Valley and the Wye Valley are particularly scenic, offering opportunities for leisurely walks, wildlife spotting, and exploration of charming towns like Crickhowell and Hay-on-Wye.

Waterfalls are another highlight of Brecon Beacons National Park. The area is home to numerous cascades, including the popular Henrhyd Falls and the enchanting Sgwd yr Eira, where visitors can walk behind the curtain of water. These natural wonders provide a refreshing respite and create picturesque settings for photography.

In addition to its stunning landscapes, Brecon Beacons National Park is known for its rich biodiversity. The park is home to a variety of wildlife, including rare species like the red kite, peregrine falcon, and otter. Keep an eye out for the ponies and sheep that graze the open moorlands, adding to the park's rural charm.

The park offers a range of outdoor activities beyond hiking and climbing. Mountain biking, horseback riding, and canoeing are popular pursuits, allowing visitors to explore the park's diverse terrain and waterways. The tranquil reservoirs of Pontsticill and Llangorse Lake provide opportunities for boating and fishing.

For those interested in history and culture, the park is dotted with ancient monuments, including prehistoric burial sites, Roman fortresses, and medieval castles. The ruins of Carreg Cennen Castle, perched on a limestone crag, offer a glimpse into Wales' turbulent past and provide breathtaking views of the surrounding countryside.

Brecon Beacons National Park offers a range of accommodation options, from cozy cottages and traditional inns to campsites and luxury hotels. The park also hosts a variety of events and festivals throughout the year, celebrating the region's natural beauty, culture, and outdoor activities.

Whether you're seeking adventurous outdoor pursuits, tranquil walks in nature, or a journey through Wales' history and heritage, Brecon Beacons National Park promises an unforgettable experience immersed in the beauty of the Welsh countryside.

5.2 Swansea and the Gower Coast:

Swansea, located on the south coast of Wales, is a vibrant city that offers a perfect blend of urban charm and stunning natural beauty. Just a short distance from Swansea lies the Gower Peninsula, a designated Area of Outstanding Natural Beauty. Here's a detailed paragraph about Swansea and the Gower Coast: Swansea, often referred to as the "Waterfront City," is a bustling metropolis that offers a mix of modern amenities, historical attractions, and a vibrant arts and culture scene. The city's waterfront area, known as Swansea Bay, features a picturesque promenade where visitors can enjoy leisurely walks, bike rides, and stunning views across the bay.

One of Swansea's main attractions is the National Waterfront Museum, which showcases the city's maritime heritage and industrial history. The museum provides interactive exhibits, artifacts, and displays that highlight the importance of Swansea's port and its impact on the region's development.

A short drive from Swansea, you'll discover the Gower Peninsula, a paradise for nature lovers and beach enthusiasts. The Gower Coast boasts some of the most beautiful and unspoiled beaches in Wales, with golden sands, crystal-clear waters, and dramatic cliffs. Rhossili Bay, often voted one of the best beaches in the world, offers breathtaking views and a vast expanse of sand, perfect for beach walks and picnics.

WALES TRAVEL GUIDE 2023

The Gower Peninsula is also known for its scenic coastal walks and hiking trails. The Gower Way, a long-distance footpath, takes you through varied landscapes, including rolling hills, woodlands, and coastal paths. One popular route is the path from Rhossili to Worm's Head, a rocky outcrop that can be explored during low tide.

For history enthusiasts, the Gower Peninsula is home to several ancient sites and landmarks. The ruins of Pennard Castle and Weobley Castle provide a glimpse into the region's medieval past, while Arthur's Stone, a Neolithic burial chamber, adds an air of mystery and intrigue.

The Gower Coast offers opportunities for a range of outdoor activities, such as surfing, kayaking, and coasteering. The peninsula's rugged coastline and strong waves attract surfers from near and far, while the calm waters of Swansea Bay provide a perfect setting for water sports and sailing.

Back in Swansea, the city offers a lively arts and culture scene, with theaters, galleries, and music venues showcasing local talent and international acts. The Dylan Thomas Centre, dedicated to the famous Welsh poet, provides insights into his life and works, and hosts literary events throughout the year.

Swansea and the Gower Coast offer a unique blend of city life and natural beauty, making it an ideal destination for those seeking a diverse and memorable experience. Whether you're exploring Swansea's urban delights or immersing yourself in the stunning landscapes of the Gower Peninsula, you're sure to be captivated by the charm and allure of this coastal region.

5.3 Pembrokeshire Coast National Park:

Pembrokeshire Coast National Park, located in the southwestern part of Wales, is a captivating and diverse coastal landscape that offers breathtaking scenery, wildlife encounters, and outdoor adventures. Here's a detailed paragraph about Pembrokeshire Coast National Park:

Pembrokeshire Coast National Park encompasses a stunning stretch of coastline that spans approximately 186 miles (299 kilometers), making it the only coastal national park in the United Kingdom. The park is renowned for its dramatic cliffs, golden sandy beaches, and pristine offshore islands, creating a paradise for nature enthusiasts and outdoor enthusiasts alike.

The coastline of Pembrokeshire offers a wealth of natural beauty. From towering cliffs and secluded coves to expansive sandy beaches, there's a diverse range of landscapes to explore. The Pembrokeshire Coast Path, a long-distance walking trail that follows the entire coastline, provides breathtaking views and the opportunity to discover hidden gems along the way.

The park is home to a rich array of wildlife, both on land and in the surrounding waters. Seal colonies can be spotted along the coastline, and boat trips from places like Tenby offer the chance to witness these playful creatures up close. Puffins and other seabirds nest on the offshore islands, such as Skomer and Skokholm, creating a haven for birdwatchers.

Pembrokeshire Coast National Park offers a multitude of outdoor activities for visitors to enjoy. The rugged cliffs attract climbers looking for a challenge, while the waters around the park are perfect for kayaking, coasteering, and surfing. Boat trips and sea safaris provide opportunities to explore the marine environment and spot dolphins, whales, and porpoises.

The park is also steeped in history and boasts several historical landmarks. Pembroke Castle, the birthplace of Henry VII, stands as an impressive fortress with its towering walls and medieval architecture. St. David's Cathedral, located in the city of St. David's, is another notable site, known for its stunning architecture and religious significance.

The coastal towns and villages within the park offer a mix of charm, history, and hospitality. Tenby, with its pastel-colored houses and sandy beaches, is a popular destination for tourists. Fishguard, a historic port town, provides a gateway to the beautiful Preseli Hills and the rugged North Pembrokeshire coastline.

Pembrokeshire Coast National Park is not just a summer destination. The park's diverse landscapes and vibrant wildlife make it an attractive place to visit throughout the year. Spring brings blooming wildflowers and bird migrations, while autumn showcases stunning coastal colors and quieter trails to explore.

Accommodation options within the park range from cozy

cottages and B&Bs to luxury hotels and campsites, ensuring that visitors have a comfortable stay while immersing themselves in the natural beauty of the area.

With its stunning coastline, rich biodiversity, and outdoor adventures, Pembrokeshire Coast National Park is a destination that truly captures the essence of Wales' coastal beauty. Whether you're seeking exhilarating outdoor activities, peaceful walks along pristine beaches, or encounters with remarkable wildlife, this national park offers an unforgettable experience for nature lovers and adventurers alike.

5.4 Tenby and its Beaches:

Tenby, a charming coastal town located in Pembrokeshire, Wales, is renowned for its picturesque harbor, historic town walls, and beautiful sandy beaches. Here's a detailed paragraph about Tenby and its beaches:

Tenby, often referred to as the "Jewel of Pembrokeshire," is a delightful seaside town that offers a perfect blend of natural beauty, historical charm, and family-friendly attractions. The town's colorful Georgian buildings, narrow streets, and medieval town walls create a unique and welcoming atmosphere.

One of the main draws of Tenby is its stunning beaches. The town boasts four main sandy beaches, each with its own distinct character. North Beach, located just below the town walls, offers a vast expanse of golden sand and is popular with families for its gentle waves and shallow waters. South Beach, stretching along the southern side of the town, is known for its long sandy stretch and panoramic views of Caldey Island.

Castle Beach, located near Tenby Castle, is a smaller beach that offers a mix of sand and pebbles. It's an excellent spot for rock pooling and exploring the fascinating marine life. Harbour Beach, nestled within the town's picturesque harbor, provides a sheltered spot for sunbathing and enjoying views of the colorful boats bobbing in the water.

Beyond the beautiful beaches, Tenby offers a range of attractions and activities. The town's medieval town walls can be explored on a leisurely walk, offering panoramic views of the coastline and surrounding countryside. The Tenby Museum and Art Gallery provide insights into the town's history, while the Tudor Merchant's House offers a glimpse into life in the 15th century.

Tenby's picturesque harbor is a hub of activity, with fishing boats, pleasure cruises, and boat trips to Caldey Island. Caldey Island, just a short boat ride away, is home to a Cistercian monastery and offers tranquil walking paths, stunning viewpoints, and beautiful beaches.

Tenby is also known for its vibrant events and festivals. The annual Tenby Arts Festival showcases local talent in music, dance, and theater, while the Tenby Summer Spectacular provides entertainment for the whole family with live music, street performances, and fireworks displays.

The town itself offers a wide range of accommodation options, including quaint guesthouses, charming bed and breakfasts, and luxury hotels with sea views. The town center is lined with a variety of shops, cafes, and restaurants, where visitors can sample delicious seafood, traditional Welsh dishes, and homemade ice cream.

Whether you're seeking relaxation on the golden sands, exploring the town's historical landmarks, or enjoying the vibrant atmosphere of the harbor, Tenby and its beautiful beaches offer a delightful coastal escape. With its scenic beauty, rich history, and warm hospitality, Tenby is a destination that captures the hearts of visitors and leaves them with lasting memories.

WALES TRAVEL GUIDE 2023

CHAPTER 6

REGION OF MIDWEST WALES

6.1 Aberystwyth and its University:

Aberystwyth, a picturesque coastal town located on the west coast of Wales, is renowned for its stunning natural beauty, rich history, and the prestigious Aberystwyth University. Here's a detailed paragraph about Aberystwyth and its university:

Aberystwyth, nestled between the rolling hills of Ceredigion and the breathtaking coastline of Cardigan Bay, is a vibrant town with a unique charm. One of its main highlights is Aberystwyth University, which is known for its academic excellence and beautiful campus. Founded in 1872, the university has a rich history and offers a wide range of undergraduate and postgraduate programs across various disciplines.

The university's campus, located just a short walk from the town center, is set amidst lush greenery and offers stunning views of the sea. The Old College, a magnificent Gothic Revival building that serves as the university's main administrative center, is a prominent feature of the campus. It has a fascinating history and is open to the public, allowing visitors to explore its grand halls and learn about the university's heritage.

Aberystwyth University is highly regarded for its academic achievements and research contributions. It offers a diverse range of courses, including arts and humanities, sciences, social sciences, and business. Students benefit from the university's state-of-the-art facilities, including modern lecture theaters, research laboratories, and libraries, which provide an ideal environment for learning and discovery.

Beyond its academic reputation, Aberystwyth University is known for its active student community and vibrant cultural scene. The town itself offers a variety of amenities, including shops, cafes, restaurants, and a lively nightlife. Students and visitors can explore the town's charming streets, visit art galleries and museums, and enjoy performances at the Aberystwyth Arts Centre, which hosts a diverse program of events throughout the year.

The location of Aberystwyth further adds to its appeal. With its proximity to the rugged coastline, sandy beaches, and picturesque landscapes, the town offers ample opportunities for outdoor activities and exploration. The nearby Cambrian Mountains provide a stunning backdrop for hiking, biking, and wildlife spotting, while the Cardigan Bay coastline offers opportunities for water sports, such as surfing and sailing.

Aberystwyth also boasts historical landmarks, including the ruins of Aberystwyth Castle, which offer glimpses into the town's medieval past. The Vale of Rheidol Railway, a steam train that runs from Aberystwyth to Devil's Bridge, provides a nostalgic and scenic journey through the stunning Welsh countryside.

The town's welcoming atmosphere and strong sense of community make it an attractive place to live and study. Aberystwyth University plays a significant role in the town's cultural and economic development, and its students contribute to the vibrant social fabric of the community.

Whether you're a student pursuing higher education or a visitor exploring the town's attractions, Aberystwyth offers a captivating blend of academic excellence, natural beauty, and Welsh hospitality. With its scenic surroundings, thriving cultural scene, and top-notch educational opportunities, Aberystwyth and its university provide an enriching and memorable experience for all who visit.

6.2 Powys National Park:

Powys National Park, located in the heart of Wales, is a sprawling and diverse natural playground that encompasses picturesque landscapes, charming villages, and rich biodiversity. Here's a detailed paragraph about Powys National Park:

Powys National Park covers a vast area in central Wales, offering a diverse range of landscapes and outdoor experiences. The park is characterized by rolling hills, deep valleys, tranquil lakes, and expansive forests, making it a haven for nature lovers and outdoor enthusiasts.

One of the highlights of Powys National Park is its stunning mountain ranges, including the majestic Brecon Beacons and the rugged Cambrian Mountains. These mountains provide breathtaking vistas, challenging hiking trails, and opportunities for mountain biking and rock climbing. The summit of Pen y Fan, the highest peak in southern Britain, offers panoramic views of the surrounding countryside and is a popular destination for avid hikers.

The park is also home to a network of enchanting rivers, such as the River Wye and the River Severn, which wind their way through the picturesque valleys. These waterways provide opportunities for canoeing, fishing, and peaceful riverside walks, allowing visitors to immerse themselves in the tranquility of the natural surroundings.

Powys National Park boasts a rich biodiversity, with diverse flora and fauna thriving in its varied habitats. Ancient oak woodlands, wildflower meadows, and heather-clad moorlands are home to a range of plant species, including rare orchids and vibrant wildflowers. The park is also a sanctuary for wildlife, with red kites, peregrine falcons, otters, and red deer among the many species that can be spotted in the area.

The park is dotted with charming villages and towns that offer a glimpse into the region's history and culture. Hay-on-Wye, known as the "Town of Books," is famous for its numerous bookshops and literary festivals. Crickhowell, nestled in the Usk Valley, is a picturesque town with its medieval castle and traditional market. These communities provide a warm Welsh welcome to visitors, with cozy pubs, local crafts, and a range of accommodation options.

Powys National Park is a haven for outdoor activities and adventure. Besides hiking and mountain biking, visitors can enjoy horse riding, fishing, and even gliding over the stunning landscapes. The park also hosts various events and festivals throughout the year, celebrating the region's heritage, music, and outdoor pursuits.

Accommodation options within the park range from cozy cottages and country inns to campsites and luxury hotels, catering to different preferences and budgets. These establishments often showcase the warm hospitality and local cuisine, allowing visitors to savor traditional Welsh dishes made with fresh local produce.

Powys National Park offers a tranquil and awe-inspiring escape into the natural beauty of Wales. With its breathtaking landscapes, diverse wildlife, and a range of outdoor activities, the park provides an ideal setting for exploration, relaxation, and reconnecting with nature. Whether you're seeking adventure, tranquility, or a taste of Welsh culture, Powys National Park promises an unforgettable experience for all who venture into its stunning wilderness.

6.3 Ceredigion and the Western Coast:

Ceredigion, located on the western coast of Wales, is a region known for its stunning coastline, charming seaside towns, and rich historical heritage. Here's a detailed paragraph about Ceredigion and its western coast:

Ceredigion, often referred to as Cardiganshire, encompasses a picturesque stretch of coastline along the western shores of Wales. The region offers a captivating blend of natural beauty, cultural treasures, and a laid-back coastal atmosphere. Its stunning sandy beaches, rugged cliffs, and tranquil coves make it a popular destination for beach lovers and outdoor enthusiasts alike.

One of the main attractions of Ceredigion is its pristine coastline. The area boasts a variety of beautiful beaches, including the award-winning Blue Flag beaches of Aberystwyth, Borth, and New Quay. These beaches offer golden sands, clear waters, and stunning views, providing perfect spots for sunbathing, swimming, and family picnics.

Ceredigion's coastline is also renowned for its wildlife. The region is a prime location for spotting bottlenose dolphins, which can often be seen frolicking in the waves and delighting visitors with their acrobatic displays. Boat trips and wildlife cruises from towns like New Quay offer opportunities to get up close and personal with these majestic creatures.

The towns and villages along the western coast of Ceredigion exude charm and character. Aberystwyth, a vibrant university town, offers a mix of cultural attractions, including museums, art galleries, and the stunning Aberystwyth Castle ruins. New Quay, a quaint fishing village, is famous for its colorful houses and its connections to the famous Welsh poet, Dylan Thomas. Visitors can explore its picturesque harbor, take boat trips, or simply relax in one of the waterfront cafes.

History enthusiasts will appreciate the rich historical heritage of Ceredigion. The region is home to several ancient castles, such as Cardigan Castle and Cilgerran Castle, which stand as reminders of the area's turbulent past. The Iron Age hillforts of Pen Dinas and Castell Bach offer glimpses into the region's ancient origins. Ceredigion also boasts a network of scenic walking and cycling trails, allowing visitors to immerse themselves in the region's natural beauty. The Ceredigion Coast Path, a long-distance trail that follows the coastline, offers breathtaking views of the sea and cliffs, with opportunities to spot wildlife and explore hidden coves along the way. Inland, the rolling hills and valleys provide ample opportunities for hiking, horse riding, and exploring the region's rural landscapes.

The region's culinary scene is influenced by its coastal location, with fresh seafood being a highlight. Visitors can enjoy delicious fish and chips, locally caught seafood platters, and traditional Welsh dishes made with locally sourced ingredients. The coastal towns also offer a range of charming pubs, cafes, and restaurants, where visitors can indulge in a leisurely meal while enjoying views of the sea.

Ceredigion's western coast provides a perfect blend of natural beauty, cultural heritage, and coastal charm. Whether you're seeking relaxation on the sandy beaches, exploring historical sites, or embarking on outdoor adventures, Ceredigion offers a welcoming and diverse coastal experience. With its stunning landscapes, rich history, and warm Welsh hospitality, Ceredigion invites visitors to discover the magic of its western coast and create unforgettable memories.

6.4 Builth Wells and Its Attractions:

WALES TRAVEL GUIDE 2023

Builth Wells, a charming market town located in the heart of Wales, offers a delightful blend of natural beauty, historical sites, and cultural attractions. Here's a detailed paragraph about Builth Wells and its attractions:

Builth Wells, situated on the banks of the River Wye in Powys County, is a picturesque town known for its peaceful atmosphere and stunning surroundings. The town's main attraction is the Royal Welsh Showground, which hosts the prestigious Royal Welsh Show every July. This agricultural show draws visitors from far and wide, showcasing the best of Welsh farming, livestock, and rural traditions.

Aside from the Royal Welsh Showground, Builth Wells boasts a rich historical heritage. The town is home to Builth Castle, a Norman fortress that dates back to the 12th century. Although now in ruins, the castle still retains its grandeur and offers a glimpse into its medieval past. Visitors can explore the remnants of the castle, including its impressive defensive walls and towers, and enjoy panoramic views of the surrounding countryside.

For those seeking natural beauty, Builth Wells is surrounded by stunning landscapes. The nearby Elan Valley, known for its reservoirs and picturesque scenery, offers opportunities for walking, cycling, and wildlife spotting. The tranquil River Wye, which runs through the town, is perfect for fishing or simply enjoying a peaceful riverside walk.

Builth Wells is also a hub for arts and culture. The Wyeside Arts Centre, housed in a converted chapel, hosts a diverse program of films, performances, and exhibitions throughout the year. The center offers a space for local artists and performers to showcase their talents, adding vibrancy to the town's cultural scene.

The town itself has a range of charming independent shops, cafes, and traditional pubs, where visitors can experience warm Welsh hospitality and sample local delicacies. The weekly market, held in the town center, is a great place to browse local produce, crafts, and antiques, providing a glimpse into the vibrant community of Builth Wells.

Builth Wells is also a gateway to the beautiful surrounding countryside. Outdoor enthusiasts can explore the nearby Brecon Beacons National Park, which offers stunning landscapes, hiking trails, and opportunities for outdoor adventures. The park's mountains, waterfalls, and rolling hills provide a breathtaking backdrop for activities such as mountain biking, horse riding, and nature walks.

Throughout the year, Builth Wells hosts various events and festivals that showcase the town's unique character and community spirit. From agricultural shows to music festivals, there is always something happening that brings locals and visitors together in celebration.

Whether you're interested in history, natural beauty, or cultural experiences, Builth Wells offers a delightful escape in the heart of

WALES TRAVEL GUIDE 2023

Wales. With its rich heritage, stunning surroundings, and warm community atmosphere, the town invites visitors to immerse themselves in its charm and create lasting memories.

CHAPTER 7

CULTURE AND LOCAL TRADITION

7.1 The Welsh Language:

The Welsh language, also known as Cymraeg, holds a significant place in the cultural identity of Wales. Here's a detailed paragraph about the Welsh language:

The Welsh language is an ancient Celtic language that has been spoken in Wales for centuries. It is a source of pride and a symbol of Welsh culture and heritage. Welsh is a living language, spoken by a substantial number of people in Wales, and it holds official status alongside English.

Welsh is a fascinating language with its own distinct sounds, grammar, and vocabulary. It is a member of the Brythonic branch of the Celtic languages, which also includes Breton and Cornish. The language has evolved over time, with influences from Latin, English, and other languages, but it has managed to retain its unique character.

Efforts to revitalize and promote the Welsh language have been successful in recent years. Welsh-medium education is available across Wales, providing children with the opportunity to learn and use Welsh as their primary language of instruction. There are also Welsh-language television channels, radio stations, and newspapers, offering a range of media in Welsh.

The Welsh language plays an important role in everyday life in Wales. While many people are bilingual and use both Welsh and English, there are communities where Welsh is the predominant language. These areas, known as Welsh-speaking heartlands, provide a vibrant setting for the language to thrive.

Welsh is not only spoken but also celebrated through literature, poetry, music, and performing arts. Welsh poets, such as Dylan Thomas and R.S. Thomas, have made significant contributions to the literary world, and Welsh-language music festivals showcase the talents of Welsh musicians and singers. Eisteddfodau, traditional cultural festivals, are held annually, where people come together to celebrate Welsh language, music, and arts.

Visitors to Wales may encounter the Welsh language in various forms. Bilingual signage is common throughout the country, and place names often retain their Welsh names alongside English translations. Learning a few basic Welsh phrases can enhance the travel experience and show respect for the local culture.

The Welsh language is more than just a means of communication; it represents a connection to Wales' history, culture, and identity. It is a living testament to the resilience and pride of the Welsh people. Embracing the Welsh language during a visit to Wales can deepen one's understanding of the country and foster a greater appreciation for its rich cultural tapestry.

7.2 Traditional Music and Dance:

Traditional music and dance hold a special place in the cultural heritage of Wales, reflecting the rich traditions and storytelling customs of the Welsh people. Here's a detailed paragraph about traditional music and dance in Wales:

Traditional Welsh music is deeply rooted in the country's history and has been passed down through generations. It is characterized by its distinctive melodies, heartfelt lyrics, and the use of traditional instruments. The harp, which is recognized as the national instrument of Wales, has been played for centuries and is associated with Welsh cultural identity. Other traditional instruments include the fiddle, accordion, flute, and the triple harp.

Vocal music is an integral part of the Welsh musical tradition. The Welsh male voice choirs are renowned worldwide for their powerful and harmonious performances. These choirs, with their deep, resonant voices, often sing traditional hymns, folk songs, and anthems, creating a powerful and emotive musical experience.

Cerdd dant, or "string music," is a unique form of traditional Welsh singing. It involves the combination of harp music with vocal poetry. The singer, known as the "cerddor," performs intricate melodies that follow the structure of the poetry, creating a beautiful and melodic interplay between the voice and the harp. Traditional Welsh folk dances are lively and energetic, often accompanied by live music. The most well-known dance is the twmpath, a social dance performed in a circle or in pairs. Participants follow a set of steps and movements, creating a joyful and communal atmosphere. Other traditional dances include the hornpipe and the reel, which showcase intricate footwork and quick movements.

Music and dance are celebrated through various festivals and events across Wales. The National Eisteddfod, a week-long cultural festival, features competitions in traditional music and dance, where performers showcase their skills and talents. Folk festivals and local community gatherings also provide opportunities to experience traditional music and dance firsthand.

Traditional music and dance play a significant role in preserving Welsh cultural heritage and creating a sense of community and pride. They provide a means of storytelling, expressing emotions, and connecting with the past. Whether through the soul-stirring harmonies of a male voice choir, the enchanting melodies of the harp, or the lively footwork of traditional dances, traditional music and dance offer a captivating glimpse into the heart and soul of Wales.

7.3 Festivals and Cultural Events:

Wales is a land of vibrant cultural festivals and events that celebrate the country's rich heritage, traditions, and artistic expressions. Here's a detailed paragraph about festivals and cultural events in Wales:

Wales hosts a wide array of festivals and cultural events throughout the year, offering a diverse range of experiences for locals and visitors alike. The National Eisteddfod stands as one of the most significant cultural festivals in Wales. This week-long event showcases Welsh music, literature, drama, dance, and visual arts, attracting participants and spectators from all corners of the country. The festival culminates in the crowning of the Bard, a poet considered the winner of the prestigious Eisteddfod Chair.

Another notable festival is the Hay Festival of Literature and the Arts, held annually in the charming town of Hay-on-Wye. Renowned authors, poets, and intellectuals from around the world gather to share their insights and engage in discussions on literature, politics, and culture. The festival's program also includes live music performances, comedy shows, and activities for children, creating a lively and intellectually stimulating atmosphere.

Music lovers will revel in the various music festivals that take place throughout Wales. The Brecon Jazz Festival brings together acclaimed jazz musicians from across the globe, attracting jazz enthusiasts and creating a lively atmosphere in the picturesque town of Brecon. The Green Man Festival, set against the backdrop of the Brecon Beacons National Park, showcases an eclectic mix of music genres, featuring both established and emerging artists. For those interested in the arts, the Cardiff International Film Festival is a must-attend event. It showcases a diverse range of international films, including feature films, documentaries, and short films. The festival provides a platform for emerging filmmakers and offers film enthusiasts the opportunity to engage with thought-provoking and inspiring cinematic works.

The Urdd National Eisteddfod is a significant festival celebrating Welsh culture and youth talent. It focuses on showcasing the artistic abilities of young people in Wales, with competitions in singing, dancing, poetry recitation, and other performance arts. The event fosters a sense of pride and achievement among the younger generation and encourages their involvement in preserving Welsh cultural traditions.

In addition to these major festivals, Wales also hosts numerous local and community events throughout the year. These range from agricultural shows and food festivals to traditional folk music gatherings and historical reenactments. These events provide a platform for local artisans, musicians, and performers to showcase their talents and contribute to the vibrant cultural fabric of Wales.

Attending festivals and cultural events in Wales offers a unique opportunity to immerse oneself in the country's rich heritage and artistic expressions. It allows visitors to connect with the local community, experience traditional music, dance, literature, and arts, and gain a deeper understanding of Welsh culture and identity. Whether you're interested in literature, music, film, or community celebrations, Wales has a festival or cultural event that will captivate and inspire you.

CHAPTER 8

TYPICAL FOOD AND DRINK

8.1 Traditional Welsh Dishes:

Welsh cuisine is deeply rooted in the country's agricultural heritage and showcases a range of hearty and flavorsome dishes. Here's a detailed paragraph about traditional Welsh dishes:

Traditional Welsh cuisine draws inspiration from the bountiful land and sea surrounding Wales. One iconic dish is Welsh rarebit, a savory delight made from a blend of cheese, mustard, and ale, spread on toasted bread and grilled until golden and bubbling. Another popular dish is cawl, a hearty soup traditionally made with lamb or beef, along with seasonal vegetables like potatoes, leeks, carrots, and swedes. Cawl is often enjoyed as a comforting meal during the colder months.

Wales is known for its excellent lamb, and a traditional favorite is roast lamb with all the trimmings. Succulent Welsh lamb, slow-roasted to perfection, is typically served with crispy roast potatoes, seasonal vegetables, mint sauce, and rich gravy. This dish exemplifies the farm-to-table ethos and showcases the quality and flavor of Welsh lamb.

Seafood lovers will relish the taste of Welsh cockles and laverbread. Cockles, small edible mollusks, are typically steamed and enjoyed as a snack or incorporated into dishes like traditional Welsh breakfasts. Laverbread, made from seaweed, is often fried with bacon and served as part of a full Welsh breakfast or as a side dish. It is a unique and distinctive flavor that reflects the coastal heritage of Wales.

Another beloved Welsh dish is bara brith, a delicious fruit loaf made with a mixture of dried fruits, spices, and tea-soaked bread. The loaf is moist and packed with flavor, often served sliced and spread with butter. Bara brith is a traditional teatime treat and a popular choice in cafes and tearooms across Wales.

Cheese plays a prominent role in Welsh cuisine, and one famous variety is Caerphilly cheese. This crumbly white cheese is often enjoyed on its own or used in dishes like Welsh rarebit and cheese platters. Another notable cheese is the creamy and distinctively flavored Welsh cheddar, produced in various regions across Wales.

To satisfy your sweet tooth, Welsh cakes are a must-try delicacy. These small, round, griddle-cooked cakes are made with flour, sugar, butter, and dried fruit. They are often enjoyed warm, dusted with sugar, and paired with a cup of tea. Welsh cakes are a delicious treat and a beloved symbol of Welsh culinary heritage. When visiting Wales, be sure to explore local markets, farm shops, and restaurants to discover an array of traditional Welsh dishes. From the comforting flavors of cawl and roast lamb to the unique tastes of laverbread and bara brith, traditional Welsh cuisine offers a delightful culinary journey that reflects the country's rich heritage and natural abundance.

8.2 Welsh Coffee and Tea:

Welsh coffee and tea culture reflects the country's love for warm beverages and socializing. Here's a detailed paragraph about Welsh coffee and tea traditions:

In Wales, coffee and tea are cherished beverages that play a significant role in daily life. When it comes to coffee, Welsh cafes and coffee shops offer a wide variety of options, from classic espresso-based drinks to artisanal creations. You can savor a perfectly brewed cappuccino, indulge in a rich and velvety latte, or enjoy the strong and aromatic flavors of a Welsh coffee, which is a delightful blend of coffee, dark rum, sugar, and topped with whipped cream. Welsh coffee is often enjoyed as a comforting after-dinner drink or during festive occasions.

Tea holds a special place in Welsh culture, with a tradition that dates back centuries. Welsh tea is typically served hot and strong, accompanied by a variety of delicious treats. One popular Welsh tea specialty is the Bara Brith, a traditional fruit loaf made with dried fruits, spices, and tea-infused flavors. This moist and flavorful loaf is often sliced and served with a spread of butter, making it a perfect accompaniment to a cup of tea.

Welsh tea rooms and cafes are renowned for their warm and welcoming ambiance. They offer a cozy atmosphere where locals and visitors can relax, catch up with friends, and enjoy a steaming pot of tea. Traditional Welsh afternoon tea is a cherished experience, featuring a selection of sandwiches, freshly baked scones with clotted cream and jam, and a tempting assortment of cakes and pastries.

In recent years, Wales has seen a rise in specialty tea shops that showcase a wide range of teas from around the world. These shops offer an extensive selection of loose-leaf teas, allowing tea enthusiasts to explore different flavors and aromas. From classic black teas to green teas, herbal infusions, and unique blends, there is something to suit every palate.

Welsh coffee and tea culture extends beyond the walls of cafes and tea rooms. Many local communities organize coffee mornings and tea parties as social events, bringing people together over a shared love for warm beverages and friendly conversations. These gatherings often include homemade cakes, pastries, and traditional Welsh treats, creating a sense of community and camaraderie.

Whether you prefer a robust cup of coffee or a comforting pot of tea, Wales has a rich coffee and tea culture that invites you to indulge in the warmth and flavors of these beloved beverages. So, take a moment to savor a Welsh coffee or enjoy a leisurely cup of tea, and immerse yourself in the delightful traditions of Welsh coffee and tea culture.

8.3 Local Specialty Products:

Wales boasts a diverse range of locally produced specialty products that showcase the country's natural resources and culinary traditions. Here's a detailed paragraph about typical local products in Wales:

Wales is renowned for its high-quality dairy products, and one iconic specialty is Welsh cheese. From the creamy Caerphilly and tangy Red Leicester to the rich and crumbly Welsh cheddar, the country offers a wide variety of artisanal cheeses. Produced by skilled cheesemakers using traditional methods, these cheeses exhibit distinct flavors and textures that have gained recognition both nationally and internationally.

Welsh lamb is celebrated for its exceptional flavor and tenderness. The lush green pastures of Wales provide ideal grazing conditions, resulting in high-quality, succulent lamb. Farmers take pride in rearing their lambs using sustainable and ethical practices, ensuring the highest standards of animal welfare. Whether enjoyed in a traditional Sunday roast or as the centerpiece of a hearty stew, Welsh lamb is a true culinary delight.

Seafood plays a significant role in Welsh cuisine, and the coastal regions offer an abundance of fresh and flavorsome catches. Cardigan Bay prawns, known locally as Cennin Aur, are renowned for their sweet taste and delicate texture. These succulent prawns are harvested sustainably from the pristine waters of Cardigan Bay and are highly sought after by seafood enthusiasts.

Welsh honey is another prized local product. The country's diverse landscapes, filled with wildflowers and heather, provide a rich source of nectar for bees. Welsh honey is known for its distinct floral notes and varying flavors depending on the region. It is often used as a natural sweetener, drizzled over desserts, or enjoyed simply spread on warm toast.

Traditional Welsh cakes, made with love and skill, are a beloved local treat. These small, round griddle cakes are crafted using a simple blend of flour, sugar, butter, and dried fruit. They are traditionally cooked on a hot griddle, resulting in a slightly crisp exterior and a soft, delicious center. Welsh cakes are commonly enjoyed with a dusting of sugar and a cup of tea, making them a quintessential part of Welsh teatime.

The craft beer scene in Wales has also been thriving in recent years. The country is home to numerous independent breweries that produce a wide range of unique and flavorful beers. From hop-forward IPAs to rich stouts and refreshing ales, Welsh breweries offer something to suit every beer enthusiast's taste.

When exploring Wales, be sure to visit local farmers' markets, artisanal food shops, and specialty stores to discover an array of regional products. From the distinctive flavors of Welsh cheese and lamb to the sweetness of Welsh honey and the traditional charm of Welsh cakes, these local specialties provide a true taste of Wales and offer a delightful culinary experience for visitors.

WALES TRAVEL GUIDE 2023

RHYS HUGES

WALES TRAVEL GUIDE 2023

CHAPTER 9

OUTDOOR ACTIVIES

9.1 Trekking and Hiking in Wales:

Wales is a paradise for outdoor enthusiasts, offering breathtaking landscapes and a plethora of hiking trails that cater to all levels of experience. Here's a detailed paragraph about trekking and hiking in Wales:

With its rugged mountains, rolling hills, dramatic coastlines, and pristine national parks, Wales provides an ideal playground for trekking and hiking adventures. One of the most popular destinations is Snowdonia National Park, home to Mount Snowdon, the highest peak in Wales. Hiking to the summit of Snowdon is a challenging but rewarding experience, with several trails to choose from, including the famous Snowdon Ranger Path and the Pyg Track. The panoramic views from the summit are truly awe-inspiring.

Another renowned hiking destination is the Brecon Beacons National Park, known for its diverse landscapes and stunning vistas. Here, you can explore the challenging trails of Pen y Fan, the highest peak in southern Britain, or opt for more leisurely walks through picturesque valleys, ancient woodlands, and sparkling waterfalls. The park offers a range of trails suitable for all abilities, including the popular Four Falls Trail and the Beacons Way.

The Pembrokeshire Coast National Park is a haven for coastal hiking enthusiasts. This rugged and beautiful stretch of coastline features the Pembrokeshire Coast Path, a long-distance trail that spans 186 miles (299 km). Along the way, you'll encounter breathtaking cliffs, secluded coves, sandy beaches, and charming coastal villages. The path is divided into manageable sections, allowing hikers to explore different segments and experience the stunning scenery at their own pace.

For those seeking a unique hiking experience, the Isle of Anglesey offers the Anglesey Coastal Path. This 130-mile (209 km) trail circles the entire island, showcasing its stunning coastal beauty and rich wildlife. From rocky headlands and sandy bays to ancient ruins and picturesque lighthouses, the Anglesey Coastal Path is a fantastic way to immerse yourself in the island's natural and cultural heritage.

Wales is also home to numerous other hiking trails and nature reserves, each with its own unique charm. The Offa's Dyke Path, a long-distance trail that runs along the border between Wales and England, offers stunning views of the countryside and historic landmarks. The Glyndŵr's Way, named after the Welsh rebel leader Owain Glyndŵr, takes you through remote landscapes and ancient forests, providing a sense of tranquility and solitude.

When embarking on a hiking adventure in Wales, it's essential to come prepared with suitable gear, including sturdy footwear, weatherproof clothing, and navigation tools. It's also advisable to check the weather conditions, inform someone about your planned route, and adhere to safety guidelines.

Trekking and hiking in Wales not only offer physical challenges and breathtaking vistas but also provide an opportunity to connect with nature, appreciate the country's rich cultural heritage, and experience the warm hospitality of local communities along the way. Whether you're a seasoned hiker or a beginner, Wales offers an abundance of trails and natural wonders that will leave you with unforgettable memories of your outdoor adventure.

9.2 Cycling and Mountain Biking in Wales:

Wales is a haven for cycling and mountain biking enthusiasts, offering a wide range of terrains, scenic routes, and thrilling trails. Here's a detailed paragraph about cycling and mountain biking in Wales:

Cycling in Wales provides a fantastic way to explore the diverse landscapes and picturesque countryside. From leisurely family rides to challenging mountainous routes, there is something for cyclists of all abilities. The country offers an extensive network of cycling paths and dedicated routes, including the popular Lon Las

Cymru (Welsh National Cycle Route), which stretches across the entire country from north to south. This long-distance trail takes cyclists through stunning scenery, charming villages, and historic sites, offering a true taste of Wales.

For mountain biking enthusiasts, Wales is a paradise. The rugged terrain, forested hills, and purpose-built mountain bike trails make it an ideal destination for adrenaline-pumping off-road adventures. Coed-y-Brenin Forest Park, located in Snowdonia, is one of the most renowned mountain biking centers in Wales. It boasts a variety of trails, ranging from family-friendly routes to technical singletracks that challenge even the most experienced riders.

Afan Forest Park in the south of Wales is another popular mountain biking destination. It offers a range of exhilarating trails, including the famous Penhydd and Skyline trails, known for their thrilling descents and technical sections. The park's diverse landscapes, including open moorland and dense forests, provide a stunning backdrop for mountain biking adventures.

In the heart of the Brecon Beacons, BikePark Wales awaits avid mountain bikers. This purpose-built facility features a network of downhill trails, jump lines, and technical descents, catering to riders of all skill levels. BikePark Wales offers shuttle services, bike rentals, and expert coaching, making it an accessible and exciting destination for mountain biking enthusiasts.

Wales also hosts a range of mountain biking events and races throughout the year. These events attract both professionals and amateurs, providing opportunities to test skills, compete, and celebrate the vibrant mountain biking community in Wales.

Cyclists and mountain bikers in Wales are not only rewarded with thrilling rides but also with stunning natural landscapes, rich wildlife, and warm Welsh hospitality. With an abundance of cycling-friendly accommodations, bike shops, and facilities, Wales ensures that riders have all they need for an enjoyable and memorable cycling experience.

Whether you're seeking a leisurely ride through picturesque countryside or an adrenaline-fueled mountain biking adventure, Wales offers a wealth of opportunities for cyclists and mountain bikers to explore its natural beauty and experience the thrill of two-wheeled exploration.

9.3 Water Sports in Wales:

Wales is a fantastic destination for water sports enthusiasts, offering a diverse range of activities along its stunning coastline, lakes, and rivers. Here's a detailed paragraph about water sports in Wales:

With over 1,200 kilometers of coastline, Wales provides ample opportunities for water sports adventures. Surfing is particularly popular, with several world-class surf breaks attracting surfers from around the globe. The Gower Peninsula, home to Rhossili

Bay and Llangennith Beach, offers excellent surfing conditions for all skill levels. Pembrokeshire, with its rugged coastline and consistent swells, is another favorite surfing destination. Whether you're a seasoned pro or a beginner, there are surf schools and rental facilities available to help you make the most of your surfing experience.

Kayaking and canoeing enthusiasts will be spoiled for choice in Wales. The country's lakes, rivers, and estuaries offer serene and picturesque settings for paddling adventures. The River Wye, flowing through the borderlands of Wales and England, is a popular spot for canoeing, with its gentle currents and beautiful scenery. The Menai Strait, separating Anglesey from mainland Wales, provides an exciting kayaking experience, where you can navigate through tidal currents and admire the stunning coastal landscapes.

Coasteering is a thrilling water activity that combines rock scrambling, cliff jumping, and swimming along the rugged coastline. Wales is regarded as the birthplace of coasteering, and it offers numerous spots where you can experience this exhilarating adventure. The Pembrokeshire Coast is a prime location for coasteering, with its dramatic cliffs, hidden coves, and crystal-clear waters providing the perfect playground for exploration and adrenaline-fueled jumps.

Sailing and yachting enthusiasts can take advantage of Wales' many marinas and sailing clubs. The picturesque harbors of

Tenby, Aberystwyth, and Cardiff offer opportunities for both leisurely coastal cruising and competitive racing. The Isle of Anglesey, with its stunning coastline and sheltered bays, is a favored destination for sailing enthusiasts.

For those seeking a more relaxed water activity, fishing in Wales is a popular pastime. The country's rivers and lakes are teeming with trout, salmon, and coarse fish, providing excellent opportunities for fly fishing and angling. Fishing permits and guides are available to help visitors navigate the best spots and ensure a successful fishing experience.

Wales also offers opportunities for diving, paddleboarding, wakeboarding, and more. The country's diverse waterways and natural landscapes provide a playground for water sports enthusiasts of all ages and skill levels.

Whether you're looking for adrenaline-pumping adventures or a peaceful day on the water, Wales has something to offer every water sports enthusiast. With its breathtaking coastlines, pristine lakes, and vibrant waterways, the country invites you to dive in, paddle out, and experience the thrill and tranquility of water sports in Wales.

9.4 Parks and Gardens in Wales:

Wales is home to a wide array of parks and gardens, offering visitors a chance to immerse themselves in nature's beauty and tranquility. Here's a detailed paragraph about parks and gardens in Wales:

Wales boasts an abundance of parks and gardens that showcase the country's rich natural heritage and horticultural splendor. One of the most renowned is Bodnant Garden, located in Conwy County. Spanning over 80 acres, Bodnant Garden offers a breathtaking collection of plants, including rare and exotic species. Visitors can explore its themed gardens, such as the Italianate Terraces, the tranquil Lily Terrace, and the beautiful Dell with its waterfalls and woodland walks.

Powis Castle and Gardens, situated in Powys, is another remarkable destination. The castle's stunning gardens feature intricately designed terraces, vibrant flower borders, and manicured lawns. The world-famous yew hedges create a sense of grandeur and charm, while the exotic and tender plants in the Orangery offer a delightful display of colors and scents.

In the heart of Cardiff, Bute Park provides a green oasis within the bustling city. This expansive park encompasses over 130 acres and features meandering paths, picturesque bridges, and beautifully landscaped gardens. Visitors can stroll along the River Taff, admire the diverse plantings in the Arboretum, or relax amidst the serene surroundings.

The National Botanic Garden of Wales, located in Carmarthenshire, is a horticultural gem. It showcases a wide range of themed gardens, including the Double Walled Garden, the Japanese Garden, and the Mediterranean Garden. The iconic

Great Glasshouse, the largest single-span glasshouse in the world, is a must-visit, housing a diverse collection of plants from around the globe.

For those seeking a truly enchanting experience, Portmeirion Village and Gardens in Gwynedd is a captivating destination. Designed in the style of an Italian village, Portmeirion features stunning architecture, colorful buildings, and lush gardens. Visitors can wander through the exotic plants and take in the picturesque views of the estuary and surrounding woodlands.

In addition to these notable gardens, Wales is dotted with numerous public parks and green spaces. Singleton Park in Swansea, Victoria Park in Cardiff, and Belle Vue Park in Newport are just a few examples of well-maintained parks that offer opportunities for leisurely walks, picnics, and outdoor activities.

Wales' parks and gardens not only provide scenic beauty but also serve as havens for wildlife, promoting biodiversity and environmental conservation. Many of these sites host events, festivals, and workshops throughout the year, allowing visitors to engage with nature, learn about gardening, and appreciate the wonders of the natural world.

Whether you're a passionate gardener, a nature lover, or simply seeking a peaceful retreat, Wales' parks and gardens offer a delightful escape into serene and captivating landscapes. So, take a leisurely stroll, marvel at the vibrant blooms, and revel in the tranquility of these picturesque settings in Wales.

CHAPTER 10

USEFUL NUMBERS AND CONTACT FOR THE TRIP

10.1 Useful Information for Visitors:

When planning a trip to Wales, it's important to have some practical information at hand to ensure a smooth and enjoyable visit. Here's a detailed paragraph with useful information for visitors:

1. Currency and Money Matters: The currency in Wales is the British Pound (£). Cash is widely accepted, and ATMs are

readily available in cities and towns. Credit and debit cards are widely accepted, but it's always handy to have some cash on hand, especially when visiting smaller establishments or rural areas.

2. Language: The official languages of Wales are English and Welsh. While English is widely spoken throughout the country, especially in tourist areas, you may come across some signs and public announcements in both languages. Locals appreciate any efforts made to learn a few basic Welsh phrases, but English will suffice for most interactions.

3. Weather: The weather in Wales can be changeable, so it's advisable to pack layers and be prepared for various conditions. Summers are generally mild, with average temperatures ranging from 15°C to 25°C (59°F to 77°F). Winters are cool, with temperatures ranging from 2°C to 8°C (36°F to 46°F). It's always a good idea to check the weather forecast before heading out for the day.

4. Time Zone: Wales operates on Greenwich Mean Time (GMT) during the winter months and British Summer Time (GMT+1) during daylight saving time. It's advisable to check the local time and adjust your schedule accordingly.

5. Transportation: Wales has a well-connected transportation system, including trains, buses, and taxis. The National Rail network offers services to major cities and towns, allowing for convenient travel within the

country. Buses are another popular mode of transport, particularly for reaching rural areas and smaller towns. Taxis can be found in urban areas and can be hailed on the street or booked in advance.

6. Safety: Wales is generally a safe destination for travelers. However, it's always wise to take precautions, such as keeping an eye on your belongings, avoiding isolated areas at night, and following any safety guidelines provided by local authorities. It's also recommended to have travel insurance that covers medical emergencies and trip cancellations.

7. Healthcare: Wales has a comprehensive healthcare system, and emergency medical care is accessible to all visitors. It's advisable to have travel insurance that covers medical expenses, as some treatments may require payment. Pharmacies (or chemists) are available throughout the country for minor ailments and over-the-counter medications.

8. Wi-Fi and Connectivity: Most hotels, cafes, and public places in Wales offer Wi-Fi access. Additionally, mobile network coverage is generally reliable across the country. If you require constant connectivity, consider purchasing a local SIM card or checking with your mobile service provider about international roaming options.

9. Customs and Etiquette: Welsh people are known for their

friendly and welcoming nature. It's customary to greet people with a polite "hello" or "good day." Tipping is appreciated but not always mandatory, and it's customary to leave a small tip in restaurants if the service was satisfactory. Smoking is banned in enclosed public spaces.
10. Emergency Contacts: In case of emergencies, dial 999 for police, ambulance, or fire services. For non-emergency situations, the non-emergency police contact number is 101.

By keeping these useful tips in mind, you'll be well-prepared to explore Wales and make the most of your visit. Enjoy your time in this beautiful country and embrace the warm Welsh hospitality!

12.1 Tourist Offices:

When visiting Wales, you can find helpful assistance and information at various tourist offices located throughout the country. Here are some popular tourist offices in Wales:

1. Visit Wales Information Centre (Cardiff): Located in the heart of Cardiff, this tourist office provides comprehensive information about attractions, accommodations, events, and activities in Cardiff and the surrounding areas. Address: 9-11 St Mary Street, Cardiff CF10 1TT.
2. Visit Wales Information Centre (Conwy): Situated in the historic town of Conwy, this tourist office offers guidance and resources for exploring Conwy County and North

Wales. Address: Vicarage Gardens, Rose Hill Street, Conwy LL32 8LD.

3. Visit Wales Information Centre (Caernarfon): Found within the majestic Caernarfon Castle, this tourist office provides visitors with insights into the local attractions, accommodations, and tours available in Caernarfon and Snowdonia. Address: Castle Ditch, Caernarfon LL55 2AY.

4. Visit Swansea Bay (Swansea): Located in Swansea's city center, this tourist office offers detailed information about the attractions, events, accommodations, and outdoor activities in the Swansea Bay area. Address: Unit 7, Plymouth Street, Swansea SA1 3QQ.

5. Visit Pembrokeshire (Haverfordwest): Situated in Haverfordwest, this tourist office is the ideal starting point for discovering the stunning coastline, historic sites, and nature reserves of Pembrokeshire. Address: Old Bridge, Quay Street, Haverfordwest SA61 2AL.

It's worth noting that there are additional tourist information centers in various towns and cities across Wales, where you can obtain brochures, maps, and personalized advice to make the most of your visit.

12.2 Emergency Numbers:

In case of emergencies, the following numbers should be dialed:

- Police: 999
- Ambulance: 999

- Fire and Rescue: 999

For non-emergency situations that still require police assistance, you can dial 101.

It's important to remember these emergency numbers and have them readily available while traveling in Wales. The emergency services are well-equipped to handle any urgent situation and provide necessary assistance when needed.